PSHE

HOME STORIES

TALKING ABOUT PERSONAL, SOCIAL AND HEALTH ISSUES AT HOME

Gordon Aspland

SOUTHGATE

Copyright © Gordon Aspland 2002
Copyright © Illustrations Southgate Publishers Ltd

First Published 2002 by Southgate Publishers Ltd

Southgate Publishers Ltd
The Square, Sandford, Crediton, Devon EX17 4LW

Printed and bound in Great Britain by Bell & Bain Ltd, Glasgow.

British Library Cataloguing in Publication Data
A CIP catalogue record for this book is available from the British
Library.

ISBN 1–85741–130–7

CONTENTS

INTRODUCTION

Schools are increasingly being given information from the DfES about issues such as Citizenship, Inclusion, Exclusion and Safety, all areas within the PSHE curriculum. How to approach these issues in practice is left to the individual school and this is where my previous books have been widely used. I have now published *Feelings*, *Choices* and *Situations* for KS2 and *Starting Out* and *First Steps* for KS1. These books have stories for assemblies that look at the many areas that concern adults and children, such as bullying, personal safety, courage, drugs, peer group pressure, respect and so on.

Home Stories is different in that the stories are intended to be read by children with their parents. Some of the stories have been trialled with Year 1 and 2 children. I have found that the reading age for average ability children is about 7/8 but the stories would interest most children between 5 and 8, i.e. Years 1 to 4. I have had a very positive response from parents, who have said that the work was 'much more interesting than the usual spellings'! Time taken varied between 10 and 20 minutes depending on how much follow-up discussion was generated.

The broad areas covered by the stories are:

BULLYING: by excluding (story 1); by name calling (story 5); and by physical violence (story 17).

FEELINGS: towards friends (stories 2 and 14); towards parents (stories 4 and 9); peer group pressure (story 4).

PERSONAL DANGER: getting lost (story 3); strangers (story 6); and drugs (story 8).

DEVELOPING PERSONAL QUALITIES: courage/self-esteem (story 7); understanding the value of money (story 4).

RELATIONSHIPS: tolerance (story 11); and controlling anger (story 10).

CITIZENSHIP: respect for nature (story 13); respect for the elderly (story 12).

HEALTH: diet and strong teeth (story 15); and headlice (story 16).

Parents may need some initial guidance and I include below some possible wording for a letter to go with the first story you send home.

The school has a programme of Personal, Social and Health Education (PSHE) which is delivered through our assemblies, class circle time and the general ethos of the school. But we feel that this is such an important area that we would like to involve parents as well.

These stories are intended for you and your child to read together. Do not worry if your child does not know some of the vocabulary. This is not a reading exercise so just tell him/her the words. The emphasis is on developing the PSHE theme in the story. Discuss with your child the issues involved and your child's feelings towards them. There are questions during the story and at the end to help you. Previous parental responses have shown that many children enjoyed revisiting the story at another time and often had different thoughts about the issues once they had been given a chance to think about them.

The story will be discussed at our next class circle time so I hope you will be able to do this by _____
Many thanks for your support.

As the letter above suggests, the best follow-up to this home activity is a circle time session when you could read the story once more and then ask for the children's views from their home discussions.

Gordon Aspland
2002

LET'S PLAY TOGETHER

Theme: excluding someone from a game

Mark always played with his best friend, Prakesh. Then one day Mark was ill and could not go to school. After two days he was better and returned to school. When he went out at playtime Prakesh was playing with Johnny. Mark asked if he could play with them but they said no.

How was Mark feeling about Prakesh now?

Mark walked around the playground on his own.

"Would you like to play with us?" asked Joanne, who was skipping with Indra and Emily. But Mark said no because he wanted to play with Prakesh.

"Mark, come and play with us," called some other children who were playing catch with a tennis ball. Mark joined in but it wasn't what he really wanted to do.

Mark was not very happy. He watched Prakesh and Johnny run around the playground. He wished he hadn't been ill. He was in a bad mood when he got home. His mother shouted at him because he wouldn't play with his sister.

The next morning he did not want to go to school. He said he was ill again but his mother didn't believe him. She made him go to school.

Why did Mark pretend he was ill?

When Mark got to school he found out that Prakesh was now ill. At playtime Johnny came up to him and asked him to play. Mark and Johnny began to chase each other around the playground. Mark forgot about Prakesh because he was having fun with Johnny.

For a few days Mark and Johnny played at break times. Then Prakesh came back. He wanted to join Mark and Johnny in their game. Johnny said no, but Mark looked at Prakesh and said …

What do you think Mark should say?

PARENTS

This is a common problem at school. It is a classic case of 'two is company but three is a crowd'. Explore with your child these questions:

1. *How does it feel to be excluded?*
2. *What should a child do if they are being excluded?*
3. *What should a child do if they see another child being excluded from a game?*

Activity:
Discuss what Mark might have said. Then talk about what happened next in the story.

THE PENCIL CASE

Theme: *feelings towards others/respect for property*

Sareena and Claire were good friends. But like many good friends they sometimes had bad days and fell out with each other. This was a bad day. On the way to school they could not agree about what game to play at break time. Claire wanted to play hopscotch but Sareena wanted to play skipping. When they met Anne at the school gate they asked her what she wanted to play. She said skipping, so Sareena was happy but Claire went off in a mood.

Do you think Claire's reaction was unfair?

Claire and Sareena sat next to each other in class and often helped each other and shared pencils. But this morning they didn't talk to each other. Claire noticed that Sareena had a new, bright red pencil case. She was obviously proud of the pencil case because she was showing it to the other children around her.

At morning break the girls went to the hall for their drink and biscuits. Sareena and Anne quickly had theirs and went outside to skip. Claire slowly ate one biscuit, watching the other girls run outside.

What was she thinking about?

She couldn't eat her second biscuit so she decided to put it into her tray and have it later with her lunch. She went into the classroom and put her biscuit away. Claire was about to leave when she noticed Sareena's pencil case on their table. She looked around and saw there was nobody else in the room. She picked up the pencil case and then searched for somewhere to hide it.

Why do you think she wanted to do this?

She dashed over to the bookcase against the wall and slipped the pencil case behind it. Then she ran outside.

When the children came back into the classroom Sareena began to search for her pencil case.

How do you think Sareena felt?

2. The Pencil Case ...

She went up to Mrs Hilton and cried, "Somebody has stolen my new pencil case!"

"I'm sure it's here somewhere," Mrs Hilton replied. "Ask some of your friends to help you look for it."

"I'll help you," said Anne.

"So will I," offered Claire.

Sareena looked gratefully at the girls. They began to search around the classroom. Claire pretended to look in a few places then she went to the bookcase.

"Here it is!" she announced.

After she had hidden the pencil case why do you think Claire wanted to find it?

"Well done, Claire," said Mrs Hilton. "I wonder how it got there? Did anybody come into the classroom during break time?" Nobody in the class said anything.

Sareena smiled at Claire when they sat down and said thank you. During the rest of the morning she shared her pencils with Claire and offered to play hop-scotch at lunch break.

When the lunch break came Claire went to her tray to get the biscuit she had saved.

"Claire, is that your morning break biscuit?" asked Mrs Hilton.

"Yes," replied Claire.

"When did you put that into your tray?" demanded Mrs Hilton.

"I came in at break time," said Claire.

"So you were in the classroom at break time when Sareena's pencil case went missing?"

"Yes," whispered Claire.

"And you were the one who found her pencil case. I think you have some explaining to do!"

What do you think Sareena felt about Claire's actions?

PARENTS

Here are some questions to discuss with your child:

1. *Why did Claire want to hide the pencil case?*
2. *At what point in the story did things go wrong for Claire? How could she have avoided this?*
3. *What should happen to Claire now?*
4. *How do you think this has affected Sareena's and Claire's friendship?*

Activity:

Explore the theme of 'do unto others as you would have them do unto you'. In other words, how would Claire feel if somebody had taken something of hers?

GETTING LOST

Theme: what to do when you get lost

Johnny had a big brother called David. Johnny liked being with David. His older brother didn't mind when they were on their own. But David was 16, and he didn't want Johnny with him when he was out with his friends. One day David was going into town with his friends to look at CDs. Johnny asked if he could come with him but David said no. Then Johnny asked his mother if he could go with David and she said yes. David was really cross about that.

Why was David cross about Johnny coming with him?

Before Johnny went out of the door his mother gave him a letter to post. Johnny put it into his pocket and chased after David. They met David's friends at the bus stop. They all ignored Johnny but Johnny didn't mind because he felt grown up being with the older boys.

When they got to the shops David and his friends went into different record shops, with Johnny following behind. Johnny was getting bored until they went into a shop that also had Play Station games. He loved his Play Station and wished he could buy a new game. He spent ages looking at the different titles. After a while he looked around for David and his friends, but they weren't there! He frantically looked around the shop but he couldn't find them.

How was Johnny feeling now?

Johnny had not been out on his own before. He stood there, not knowing what to do. He ran out of the shop to see if David was waiting for him outside but he was nowhere to be seen. He went back into the shop to have another look. But no, David was not there. Johnny began to feel frightened and upset when a friendly shop assistant asked him if he was all right. He explained that his brother had left him and he didn't know what to do. The assistant said she would telephone his mother but he didn't know the number. She asked Johnny if he knew his address so she could look it up in the telephone book but he couldn't remember it. This made him cry even more. He wondered if he would ever get home again!

Then he remembered the letter his mother had asked him to post. He took it out of his pocket. It was a post card for a competition his mother was entering. On it was not only his address but his telephone number! The assistant took the card and went to the telephone. Johnny could see that she was talking to somebody. When she finished she told Johnny to stay where he was and his mother would be with him in ten minutes. Johnny was very relieved!

PARENTS

Here are some questions to discuss with your child:
1. Who can you ask for help if you get lost?
2. How did David act irresponsibly?
3. It is very easy to get lost in a busy shop or market. What arrangement could you make in case you get separated?

Activity:
Make sure that not only does your child know his/her telephone number and address but also knows how to write them down.

THE NEW SHOES

Theme: understanding the value of money/peer group pressure

Anne didn't want the shoes her mother showed her. She didn't want the shoes her father brought her to look at. She stood in the middle of the shop and pointed at the shoes she wanted. But the trouble was they were twice the price of the other shoes.

"Why don't you like these?" asked her father.

"And what's wrong with this pair?" asked her mother.

"Nobody wears those," said Anne. "This is the pair I want. All the girls are wearing these."

Why doesn't Anne like the shoes her parents show her?

The pair of shoes Anne wanted were very expensive. Her parents didn't have a lot of money and wanted to buy Anne a cheaper pair. But Anne wanted the same as Claire and Sareena, she didn't want any other shoes. When her parents said no, she began to cry.

Was Anne being fair to her parents?

When Anne's parents saw how upset she was they gave in and bought the shoes she wanted. She was so pleased she wanted to wear them right away.

As they were leaving the shop, Anne turned to her mother and said, "You were going to buy a new pair of shoes too. Should we look for some now?"

"Good heavens, I can't afford a new pair," replied her mother.

"Why not? You need a new pair." asked Anne.

"Because, young lady, we spent all our money on your shoes. Your mother will have to wait a few months until we can save some more money," her father told her.

Anne looked down at her new shoes and suddenly she felt very guilty.

PARENTS

Anne didn't realise the monetary pressure she was putting her parents under. Here are some questions for you to discuss with your child:

1. *Why did Anne feel guilty at the end?*
2. *How did her parents show that they really cared about her?*
3. *Why does Anne want to wear the same as the other girls? Should this be important?*

Activity:

Discuss the problems of 'peer group pressure'. When is it good to be the same and when is it not?

THE NEW GIRL

Theme: bullying – saying unkind things

It was Sarah's first day at her new school. She was dreading the day because she knew what was going to happen. The other children would start teasing her about her weight. Sarah had a problem about being fat. At her last school the children called her names and laughed at her when she couldn't run well in PE. She hated getting changed because they would stare at her. She could see them pointing at her and giggling.

Why was Sarah nervous about going into her new class?

When she walked into the class she could feel the other children staring at her. A group of girls started giggling and some boys blew their cheeks out to make them look fat. It was just what Sarah was dreading. Mrs Hatch found her a seat next to one of the giggling girls, Anne. Mrs Hatch asked Anne to look after her at playtime. She knew that Anne was a popular girl in the class and if Anne befriended Sarah then so would the other girls. But Anne wasn't friendly. As soon as they all went out to play she ran off with her friends and left Sarah on her own. Nobody talked to Sarah and she could hear them make little piggy sounds.

How was Sarah feeling now?

Sarah had a dreadful day and was glad when she went home. At dinner time her mother said that somebody was coming around to their house that evening to tell them about the local church. Later in the evening Sarah was watching television when she heard the doorbell ring. She heard her mother greet the lady from the church. Her mother brought the lady into the lounge to meet her and Sarah had a real surprise. Standing next to her was Anne, the girl from her class who had been horrible to her all that day. Anne seemed to be just as surprised as Sarah! "Why don't you take Anne upstairs to play while I talk to her mum," suggested Sarah's mother.

5. The New Girl ...

The two girls went upstairs and Sarah made a real effort to be kind. She shared her Barbie dolls with Anne and they began to have a good play with them. Anne learned a lot about Sarah that evening. She learned about her weight problem and how it affected her life. She learned about how unhappy she was at her last school because the other children teased her. She learned how nice Sarah was, sharing all her toys with her. Anne began to feel really guilty about the way she had treated Sarah at school. Sarah had a problem and she needed people to help her, not make fun of her.

What do you think Anne should do the next day at school?

The next day was the beginning of a new life for Sarah. When she got to school Anne greeted her with a smiling face. Anne took her over to the other girls and told them Sarah was going to join them in their playtime games. The other girls weren't too sure about this but Anne was the leader. Over the next few days, and then weeks, the girls learned to like Sarah. No, she could never run as fast as them, but she was a nice girl who never said a bad word about anybody else. Some of the boys still teased her but Anne and the other girls would tell them off or tell their teacher. Sarah never felt lonely again and that was all that mattered to her.

PARENTS

Children can be very cruel to someone in their class for no other reason than that the child is different in some way.

1. *Explore with your child the kinds of feelings that the other person may have and what it must be like to be unpopular.*
2. *Talk about how your child could help an unpopular pupil or what they could do if they heard other children bullying this pupil by teasing them.*

Activity:

Ask your child to think about one pupil in their class who is often teased or bullied in some other way. Your child can think of a way to show some kindness to this pupil that would make them happy. How would your child feel if he/she succeeded in doing this?

THE STRANGER

Theme: saying 'No' to strangers

It was summer and the light evenings meant that Sareena could go to her friend's house on her own. Her friend was called Claire and she lived two blocks away. Sareena's mother said that she must come home at eight o'clock.

Why did Sareena's mother give her a time when she must come home?

Sareena and Claire had a nice time playing together and when it was eight o'clock Sareena said goodbye and started to walk home. She was feeling tired and didn't really notice a car stop. A man got out and stood in front of her.

"Hello," said the man. "What's your name?"

"Sareena," she said without thinking.

"My name is Bob. I'm very pleased to meet you, Sareena. I was wondering if you could help me." The man took a step forward towards Sareena. "I've lost my puppy. Do you think you could help me find it?"

"I don't know," said Sareena.

"Oh, come on, I'm sure that a bright girl like you would know where to look. He's a cute little dog and I know he would like to play with you when we find him."

Sareena began to shake with fright. She didn't know this man – he was a stranger. A policeman had once

6. The Stranger ...

visited her school and told them not to talk to strangers. It was just a story then – now it was for real!

Describe how Sareena was feeling now.

"Come on, Sareena, I really need your help. Here, I've got some sweets," said the man called Bob. He reached into his pocket and brought out a bag of sweets. "I talked to your mother and she said it would be all right to come with me."

Should Sareena believe him? What should she do?

The man took another step towards Sareena. He was nearly close enough to grab her. He was in her way so she couldn't run towards home. Then she had an idea: she turned around and started to run back to Claire's house because it was closer. She could hear the man run after her. His footsteps were sounding closer and closer. She could almost feel his heavy breathing when she reached Claire's house. She just hoped that somebody would come to the door quickly!

Just as she reached the door it opened – she couldn't believe her luck. Mr Jones, Claire's father, was putting some rubbish in the bin by the door.

"Sareena, did you forget something?" he asked. Sareena couldn't say anything, she was so frightened and she just stood there and cried. Then Mr Jones saw the man called Bob, who had stopped when the door opened. He suddenly realised what was happening. "Hey, what do you think you're doing?" he shouted.

The man turned and ran back down the road to his car and quickly drove away. Mr Jones stood there staring at the car, saying aloud the car's number. He took Sareena into the house and immediately telephoned the police to tell them what had happened. He then telephoned Sareena's mother to get her to come round and collect Sareena. It would be a while before Sareena felt safe walking out on her own again.

PARENTS

This kind of story is every parent's nightmare. We can't always be there to protect our children so we need to help them recognise the danger signals and know what to do. Discuss with your child some of these issues, such as:

1. *What did Bob say that could signal trouble?*
2. *Discuss how an adult who was genuinely looking for a dog would behave.*
3. *Some dangerous adults could be in a couple, man and woman, and look perfectly nice. But if they are strangers should you stop and talk to them?*

Activity:
Discuss the tactics your child should use if faced with this situation. For example: don't get close, don't go near the car, shout and make a lot of noise, and run!

ON THE WATER

Theme: courage to overcome fear

Johnny looked at the other children enjoying themselves. They were furiously paddling their kayaks and bashing into each other like bumper cars. He looked at their happy faces and wished he could join them. He looked at them splashing each other and racing about. He really wanted to join in but he couldn't do it. He stood there, wanting to get into his kayak, but he couldn't. He couldn't because he didn't know how to swim and he was frightened of the water.

How was Johnny feeling as he watched the others?

Prakesh and Mark paddled over to him and called out to him to join them. But he just stood there hugging his life jacket and staring at the paddle in his hand. One of the instructors, called Bruce, walked over to him and gently told him not to worry.

"Come on, Johnny, I'll be there in my kayak right beside you."

"I don't want to," said Johnny. He did really but he didn't know what to say.

"Why don't you just sit in your kayak here on the beach?" suggested Bruce.

Johnny thought about this. He agreed to do it and climbed into the boat.

"How does that feel?" asked Bruce.

"All right," said Johnny. Bruce then suggested that he pull the boat to the edge of the beach so that the kayak was just in

7. On The Water ...

the water. He said he would hold it steady. At first Johnny said no, but Bruce promised not to let go, so he agreed. Bruce gently pulled the kayak into the water and Johnny gripped his paddle tightly as he felt the little boat float.

"That's all right, isn't it?" asked Bruce. Johnny nodded and he even managed a weak smile.

What do you think was going through Johnny's mind now?

"I'll hold the boat while you practice taking a few strokes with your paddle," said Bruce.

Johnny slowly reached out and dipped his paddle into the water. He didn't fall in! He took another stroke and then another.

"That's brilliant, Johnny!" shouted Bruce. The other boys came over and also shouted encouragement by saying "well done" to him. This made Johnny feel very good and he was ready for the last stage.

"I'll let go but I'll be right beside you," said Bruce. Johnny carried on paddling and slowly his kayak began to move forward. He started to get used to the bobbing movement of the kayak and his fears began to vanish. Bruce paddled his kayak beside him and kept telling him how well he was doing. Johnny was finally enjoying himself – but he stayed clear of the game when the others were trying to tip each other in the water!

PARENTS
Johnny overcame his fear by breaking down the task into small stages. Discuss with your child the stages that Johnny went through.
1. How did his friends help him?
2. What would have happened if they had teased him instead?
3. How did Johnny show courage?

Activity:
Ask your child to think about something that frightens them. Now discuss ways they could overcome this fear.

THE SWEETS

Theme: drugs awareness

The local rec was the place where older children enjoyed hanging out. Claire, Anne and Sareena were too young to go on their own but their parents let them go to the swings area if they were together. When they got to the swings there were older children on them so they sat on the grass and waited for the others to leave. After a while an older girl, called Maria, left her swing and wandered over to the three girls.

"Anybody want a sweet?" she asked them. Sareena and Anne said no but Claire hesitated.

Should Claire accept the sweet?

"Yes please," said Claire. Maria took a plastic bag out of her pocket. In it were small oval-shaped sweets, about the size of Smarties, and coloured pink. She offered one to Claire.

"I wouldn't take one if I were you," warned Sareena.

"They look like pills not sweets," said Anne.

"Don't listen to them," sneered Maria. "I'm just trying to be friendly. They're only harmless sweets."

If they were not sweets what else could they be? How would they affect Claire?

Claire liked to think that she was as old and mature as Maria so she took the sweet.

"At least somebody isn't a sissy," sneered Maria.

8. The Sweets ...

She wandered back to her friends who all looked at Claire and giggled.

Claire sucked at the sweet. At first it tasted sweet but then it became bitter. She wanted to spit it out but not in front of Anne and Sareena. Soon she began to feel funny. Her head felt dizzy, she couldn't see properly. She tried to stand up but she fell over. She could hear Maria and her friends laughing. Anne and Sareena tried to pick her up but when they did she was sick. Claire fell to the ground again and this time she lay still. When Maria saw this she stopped laughing and ran out of the rec.

At this moment a mother was walking with her toddler towards the swings. Anne ran over to her for help. When the mother saw Claire lying on the ground she took out her mobile telephone and called an ambulance.

Claire had to stay in hospital for a couple of days. The doctors said that she had taken a strong drug, which made her ill. She was a very silly girl. The police were trying to find Maria and her friends.

PARENTS

Discuss these issues with your child:

1. **Why did Claire take the 'sweet'?**
2. **Why didn't Claire want to spit it out?**
3. **It wasn't a sweet, so what was it? (This was an ecstasy tablet, very commonly accessible to primary children.)**
4. **What should you do if you find any pills that look like sweets?**
5. **What is there in the house that could be dangerous to swallow?**

Activity:
Talk about the good things drugs do for us and why we sometimes need to take them.

CAN I GO OUT TO PLAY?

Theme: playing one parent off against the other

Prakesh was bored. It was Saturday afternoon and he wanted to go out to play. His mother had said no because he had not tidied his bedroom. He sat on his bed moving toys from one untidy pile to another. His room was not getting any tidier.

"Have you finished yet?" his mother shouted from the bottom of the stairs.

"Nearly," he shouted back. But he wasn't in the mood to tidy his room. He really wanted to go out to play with Johnny.

Why do you think his mother told him to tidy his room first?

Prakesh heard his father come home from work. He then heard his mother go out. He went downstairs. "Has Mum gone out?" he asked his father.

"Yes, she's gone to the shop to get some milk," his father replied.

"Can I go out to play?" Prakesh asked his father.

"OK," his father said from behind the newspaper.

What doesn't his father know?

Prakesh ran outside and cycled around the corner to Johnny's house. He then spent a few hours playing football with Johnny in his back garden. On the way home he remembered that it was tonight when *Star Wars* was being shown on television. He hadn't seen it yet so he was really looking forward to it. His mother asked him where he had been when he came in. When he had told her she gave him a hard look.

After dinner it was time to see *Star Wars*. As he settled in front of the television his mother came into the lounge and turned the television off!

"Mum! You said this morning I could see *Star Wars*!" said Prakesh.

"I also said you couldn't go out to play unless you tidied your room. Upstairs and do it now!"

PARENTS

Children are very good at playing one parent off against the other. Children never realise that they usually get found out! Discuss with your child these questions:

1. *Why did Prakesh ask his father if he could go out when he knew he had to clean his room first?*
2. *Talk about what 'deceitful' means. Can you trust a deceitful person?*
3. *Was Prakesh's mother fair to turn the TV off?*
4. *How does Prakesh feel about his mother's attitude towards him? Does he feel the same about his father?*

Activity:

Explore the range of feelings between Prakesh and his two parents and also the feelings between the parents. By his deceit Prakesh may have caused a bad feeling between his parents.

A BAD DAY

When Claire got to school she was in a really bad mood. Her bad day started at breakfast when she spilt orange juice over her school skirt. She then had to change into her older skirt, which was too tight for her. She was halfway to school when she realised she had left her lunch box at home. She wanted to go back home to get it but her mother said no. She didn't want Claire to be late for school and anyway, she could have a school dinner. But Claire didn't like school dinners.

How did Claire feel when she got to school? Whose fault was it?

Claire's bad day continued during the morning. She got her adding sums all wrong in Maths. Her favourite pencil broke during Literacy and she had to use an old stump of a pencil. This made her writing very untidy and her teacher told her off. By lunchtime she was really mad. She refused to eat a school dinner so she went out to play feeling hungry. Her friends, Sareena and Anne, were playing catch with a tennis ball. Anne called for Claire to join them and threw the ball to her. She dropped the ball and angrily picked it up and threw it back at Anne. The ball hit Anne in the face. Claire didn't say sorry and stomped off to sit on her own.

Is it fair that Claire should take her anger out on her friends?

After lunch the class were painting. Claire was next to Anne but she wasn't talking to her. She wasn't talking to anybody and nobody really wanted to talk to her! She dipped her brush into the paint pot but she put too much on to the brush. She dripped black paint all over her piece of paper. Claire shouted in anger and threw her brush down. The brush hit the paint pot and knocked it over. Black paint went all over the table and all over Anne's painting which was nearly finished. Claire looked at what she had done and burst into tears.

PARENTS

Some children find it difficult to control their anger. They let their frustration build up and take it out on their friends. Here are some points for discussion:

1. **When did Claire finally lose control of her actions because of her anger?**
2. **What things make you angry?**
3. **When is it all right to get angry?**
4. **How do people act badly when they get angry? What are the results of this?**
5. **If you see a friend getting angry how can you help them?**
6. **If you were Claire's friend how would you help her?**

Activity:
With your child think of ways of controlling anger. Here are two for you to discuss:
1. **Stop what you are doing, count to ten, take a deep breath or walk away until you have calmed down.**
2. **Talk to a friend, parent or teacher about what is making you angry.**

GEORGE IS SPOILING OUR GAME!

Theme: tolerance – respecting others' games

George was always spoiling other children's games. He was in the top class and especially liked spoiling younger children's fun. He would run by and grab their skipping rope and fling it into the air or jump on their hop-scotch. His favourite pastime was kicking other boys' footballs away as far as he could. Whenever the other children complained to a teacher he would always say it was an accident: the ball hit his feet when he was running by.

Why do you think George would want to spoil other people's games?

One day Johnny, Prakesh and Mark were kicking a ball to each other. George ran by and kicked their ball as hard as he could. The ball gave a loud 'pop' sound and then went flat. Mark ran after the ball. He picked it up and sadly looked at it. Johnny and Prakesh ran over to Mrs Patel, a dinner lady. They complained that George spoiled their game. Mark showed her their ball. She said that she would go into school and find another one for them to play with.

Mrs Patel went into the school. She started looking for a ball for the boys. She walked by George's classroom and she spotted a bright yellow ball in the corner under a bench. She thought it belonged to the school so she picked it up and took it outside. What she didn't know was that it actually belonged to George. He brought it to school to use at the after school football club.

Johnny, Prakesh and Mark were really pleased with the ball and thanked Mrs Patel. They started having a good game, when guess who came running by. George got to the ball before any of the other boys and gave it a mighty kick. He laughed as he watched it sail over the fence into a neighbour's garden. Mrs Patel was very cross with him.

What do you think George is going to say? Should Mrs Patel believe him?

Mrs Patel wouldn't listen to his excuses and sent him into school to report to his teacher. His teacher, Miss Roberts, was sitting at her desk. But before he started to explain what had happened he noticed that his football was missing.

PARENTS
There is often an older child like George who likes to spoil other children's games, especially younger ones. Here are some discussion points:
1. **What happened to George's ball?**
2. **How is he going to feel when he finds out what happened to his ball?**
3. **What should happen to George now?**

Activity:
One day your child and their friends will be the eldest in school. Discuss how they should behave towards younger children. They should remember what it was like having their game spoiled by older children. Discuss ways in which they could set a good example.

MR DUNCAN

Theme: respect for the elderly

Mr Duncan was an elderly man who lived on his own. He lived in the same street as Mark, but Mark never paid much attention to him. Then one day Mark and Prakesh were walking along the street. They decided to ring Mr Duncan's doorbell then run away fast. He was very old and a bit slow so by the time he reached the door they would be at the end of the street. They sneaked up to his door, rang the bell and dashed away laughing.

Why is this a cruel thing to do?

A few days later Mrs Hilton said that they were going to have a visitor. They were studying what it was like to live in the city during the war. She had arranged for an elderly person who lived locally at that time to come into the class and talk to the children. Much to Mark's and Prakesh's amazement in walked Mr Duncan. The class listened as Mr Duncan told them how he was wounded in the leg at the beginning of the war. Then, when he was home he helped put out fires caused by the bombs. He was obviously a very brave man and when he finished all the children gave him a loud clap.

How do you think Mark and Prakesh are feeling now?

Johnny asked him if his war wound still hurt. He said yes, he now had to use a stick to help him walk. He said that it hurt even more when he had to get up from his chair and keep answering the door when nobody was there. He looked straight at Mark when he said that. Mrs Hilton said that was a dreadful thing to do and she hoped nobody in her class would do such a thing. Mark looked at Prakesh, they both had very red and embarrassed faces.

On the way home Mark and Prakesh talked about Mr Duncan. They slowed down as they came to his house. They walked up to his doorbell and rang it. This time they did not run away.

What did they do or say?

> **PARENTS**
> *Here are some questions for you to discuss with your child:*
> 1. **How does Mr Duncan feel when he goes to his door and sees nobody there?**
> 2. **What should Mark and Prakesh say to Mr Duncan?**
> 3. **What kind of things could they do to help him?**
>
> **Activity:**
> *Ask your child to think about an elderly person in your family. Your child could make them happy by writing them a letter, perhaps telling them about what he/she is doing in school.*

THE BUMBLE-BEE

Theme: respect for nature

Mark really enjoyed nature study. He loved going out on walks and looking at the hedgerows to search for beetles and butterflies. He didn't touch them. He just looked up their names in a book and enjoyed watching them. He liked their colour and shape. He liked the way the beetles walked in a funny way and the way butterflies fluttered from flower to flower. So when Mrs Hilton, his teacher, suggested visiting the nature area he was really pleased.

Why was Mark pleased to visit the nature area?

Mark had to work with Adil, a new boy in the class. They went off in search of beetles hiding under the leaves. Mark was good at finding beetles and very quickly he discovered two stag beetles mating. He pointed to them, showing Adil where they were. He was just about to tell Adil what they were when Adil did something that really shocked Mark. He picked the stag beetles off the leaf and began to pull their legs off. Mark couldn't believe that anyone could be so cruel. Adil just laughed and said it was fun.

Do you think it was fun to do what Adil did?

13. The Bumble Bee ...

Mark went off to find Mrs Hilton and tell her what had happened. Meanwhile, Adil picked up a stick and began to search for other insects. He saw a bumble-bee resting on the ground. He pointed his stick at the bumble-bee and stabbed it. He then waved the stick in the air with the bumble-bee stuck on the end. Its little legs were still moving as Adil waved the end of the stick in front of other children's faces. That was when he did something which taught him a real lesson.

He saw a corner of the nature area that had been roped off. Nobody was supposed to go past the rope. Of course Adil ducked underneath the rope and peered into a bush. He thought he saw a grey paper bag with flies all around it. He poked the bag and suddenly there was a loud buzzing sound. It wasn't a bag but a wasps' nest and the wasps were very angry with Adil for poking their nest. They started to buzz around him and sting him. Adil dropped his stick and ran screaming out of the nature area. Mark saw him run away with wasps chasing him. Mark smiled to himself!

PARENTS

The episode with the bumble-bee sounds far-fetched but is based on something that really happened. It is hard to believe how cruel some children can be. Here are some points to discuss with your child:

1. *Why do you think Mark had a smile on his face?*
2. *When do we need to kill insects? (E.g. Killing flies that spread germs on to food.)*
3. *Discuss the consequences of not looking after nature. (E.g. What would happen if we destroyed one part of a foodchain, such as digging up a hedgerow where birds feed?)*

Activity:
Look at ways in which we can look after our environment. Perhaps your child could design their own nature corner. Discuss the types of plants needed in order to attract butterflies.

LOSING A FRIEND

Theme: coping when a good friend moves away

Rebecca was very upset. Her mother had just told her that her best friend, Sobia, was moving away. Her father had got a new job that meant moving house. The two girls were born in the same week at the same hospital. Their mothers had become good friends. They only lived one block away from each other so they were always visiting. Rebecca and Sobia were growing up together. They even shared birthday parties. They were very good friends, almost like sisters. But now Sobia was moving away.

How do you know the two girls were good friends?

The girls were in the same class at school and always sat next to each other. They were always together at playtimes though they did play with some of the other girls such as Anne and Sareena. Then the day came when Rebecca went to school and Sobia was no longer there.

How do you think Rebecca felt when she got to school and Sobia wasn't there?

At first Rebecca didn't want to go to school but her mother made her go. She stared at the empty seat beside her. She couldn't think about her work, she could only think about her friend. Rebecca burst into tears at the thought of not having Sobia next to her. Her teacher, Mrs Hilton, put her arm around her and reassured her that she had lots of other good friends in school.

14. Losing a Friend ...

Mrs Hilton asked Anne to sit by Rebecca during the morning. At playtime Rebecca felt lost in the playground. She kept looking around to see if Sobia was there, but she wasn't. Then Anne and Sareena came up to her and asked her to play. They had a skipping rope so Rebecca took one end and with Anne at the other, they began to turn the rope for Sareena to jump over. For a while Rebecca forgot about her best friend and the playtime went quickly. She became very quiet and sad again when she went back to class but she was able to concentrate on her work a little better.

When she got home her mother asked her if she had had a good day. She said it was horrible without Sobia. Then her mother reminded her about the day Sobia must have had. Not only missing her best friend but going into a strange school and not knowing anybody. At least Rebecca knew her teacher and had other friends to play with. Rebecca now felt very guilty because she had only been thinking about herself. She said she would telephone Sobia that evening to see how she got on.

In time Rebecca got used to not having Sobia with her. She made good friends with the other girls, especially Anne and Sareena, but she did not forget Sobia. They often phoned and learned how to e-mail each other on the computer. Sobia had only moved fifty miles away, so their parents made arrangements to meet during the holidays.

PARENTS
Losing a good friend can leave a child feeling very lonely. Here are some discussion points:
1. *Who was feeling worse, Rebecca or Sobia?*
2. *How did the other girls help Rebecca?*
3. *What could you do if you saw someone looking lonely on his or her own?*

Activity:
Talk about how good friends are very precious to us. Discuss ways we can keep in contact with our friends.
Ask your child to write a letter to a friend or relative who lives some distance away.

THE DENTIST'S VISIT

Theme: the importance of healthy eating for strong teeth

Mark's mother read the school newsletter. "I see the school dentist is coming this week," she said to Mark. "Maybe she could find out which tooth of yours is hurting."

Mark groaned. He had just told his mother about his sore tooth. He had been having toothache for a few weeks so he knew it probably meant another filling. He had a filling six months ago. It didn't hurt too much but he still didn't like it. The filling did stop his tooth from aching though.

Why doesn't Mark want to go to the dentist?

The next day at lunchtime Mark was sitting next to Prakesh. He was still thinking about the dentist. "Have you ever been to the dentist and had a filling?" he asked Prakesh.

"No, have you?"

"I had one last year," Mark replied.

"Did it hurt?" asked Prakesh.

"No, but it wasn't nice," said Mark. "My mum said I might have to go again."

What might happen to Mark's tooth if he doesn't have it seen by the dentist?

Mark's class was due to see the dentist the following afternoon. In the morning Mrs Hilton did a lesson about healthy eating, especially about foods that are bad for your

15. The Dentist's Visit ...

teeth. Mark was thinking about the lesson at lunchtime as he opened his lunch box. He looked over at Prakesh to see what he had. He could see cheese sandwiches, sticks of carrot, an apple and a carton of orange juice. Just the kind of things Mrs Hilton said were good for you.

He then looked at his own lunch box. He had a jam sandwich, crisps, chocolate biscuits and a can of cola. These were the kind of things Mrs Hilton said were bad for you, especially if you ate them every day, which he did! He also had sweets in his pocket to eat on the way home. He sometimes sneaked sweets to bed at night after he had brushed his teeth.

What was wrong with Mark's diet?

"Next please," said the nurse. Prakesh had just come out smiling. The dentist said he had very clean, strong teeth. It was Mark's turn. The dentist was quiet as she looked inside Mark's mouth and examined his teeth. She stopped once to write something down.

"Have you had any toothache recently?" she asked him.

"Yes," replied Mark.

"I don't think you've been looking after your teeth as well as you should. I think we shall need to see you at the clinic." She gave Mark a letter for his parents. It looked like he was going to have another filling!

PARENTS

Most schools include 'Looking after your teeth' as part of their Health programme. Here are some issues to discuss with your child:

1. *Why was it wrong for Mark to eat a sweet after he had brushed his teeth at night?*
2. *Give one reason why Prakesh never had toothache.*
3. *Discuss other things the dentist does besides fillings, such as straightening teeth.*

Activity:
Plan a healthy lunch box for a week.

A PROBLEM OF HEADLICE

Theme: good hygiene with hair

"You're disgusting," said Claire to Adil. A headlouse had just fallen from his head on to their table and he gleefully squashed it with his finger. He then flicked it across the table at Claire. Claire screeched and jumped out of her chair as Adil laughed.

How would you react if somebody did that to you?

"What's going on here?" asked Mrs Hilton as she walked over to their table. "You are supposed to be doing your maths."

"Adil squashed a nit on the table," said Sareena.

"And then he flicked it at me!" shrieked Claire.

"First of all it's not a nit, but a headlouse. Nits are the eggs that headlice lay," said Mrs Hilton. She stood behind Adil and peered closely at his head. His hair seemed to be infested with headlice.

"I think you had better come with me, Adil," she told him.

What does 'infested' mean?

The girls were relieved to see Adil go. He was probably going to be sent home to have his hair treated.

"I don't want headlice," said Claire.

16. A Problem of Headlice ...

"My mum said I won't get them because my hair is clean," said Sareena.

"Adil must be really dirty," replied Claire.

"Actually, headlice like all kinds of hair, and especially clean hair," said Mrs Hilton. She overheard the girls talking when she came back into the classroom. "I think you should have your hair tied up, Sareena."

Claire had very short hair but Sareena had long, black hair. She was very proud of her hair and liked to keep it loose. She didn't say anything to Mrs Hilton, but she never got headlice so she wasn't going to tie her hair up.

Why is it a good idea for children to have long hair tied up?

That evening Sareena had a bath and her mother washed her hair. As she was combing and drying it she saw bits of grit on the comb. When she looked more closely she realised that the little black dots were moving! They were headlice! Sareena's mother was shocked and Sareena couldn't believe it! Her mother searched carefully for any eggs but couldn't find any. "I know what we are going to do," her mother announced.

The following morning Sareena rather sheepishly entered the classroom. Her classmates stared at her because they had never seen her with her hair tied up!

PARENTS

Headlice are a problem that just won't go away! Here are some questions to discuss with your child:

1. *What kind of hair do headlice like?*
2. *How did Sareena's mother find the headlice?*
3. *What are nits?*

Activity:

Headlice do not jump or fly, they crawl from head to head. Discuss ways of reducing the spread of headlice from one person to another, such as tying back long hair, avoiding close contact when playing, good grooming, etc.

KICKING OUT

Theme: physical bullying

"Come on, you'll turn into a wrinkled prune if you stay in that bath any longer," said Johnny's mother. She held the towel as he climbed out of the bath.

"Good heavens, what's happened to your legs?" she asked.

Johnny looked down. His legs were covered in black and blue bruises. "That's from playing football," he replied.

"It looks like the other boys have been using you as a football! Look, one, two, three, four, five big bruises. Has someone been deliberately kicking you?"

"No, it's just football," Johnny insisted. His mother did not believe him but she did not say any more.

Johnny was not telling the truth. He was being deliberately kicked at school. Why do you think he won't tell his mother?

It was playtimes when Johnny was getting kicked. It began when the new boy, Adil, started school. Johnny was a good footballer, much better than the other boys. He could dribble the ball, pass and shoot with skill. His friends all admired his skills but Adil was jealous. He didn't like how Johnny was popular with the other boys. He didn't like how Johnny was really good at football. So to get Johnny out of the game he would kick him hard on the leg. He usually did this when the other boys weren't looking. Adil was a big boy, much bigger than Johnny. He liked to bully smaller boys, especially if he didn't like them.

17. Kicking Out ...

Why was Adil jealous of Johnny?

The day after Johnny's mother noticed his bruises Adil went too far. This time he kicked Johnny so hard that he fell to the ground clutching his leg. Mark and Prakesh, Johnny's best friends, both saw what happened. They didn't know whether Adil was deliberately kicking Johnny before, but now they knew. They glared at Adil.

"You did that deliberately," said Mark.

"You're not playing in any of our games again," added Prakesh.

"What's going on?" asked Mrs Hilton, who was on playground duty. "That's a nasty cut on your leg, Johnny. How did you get that?"

Johnny didn't have to answer because Mark and Prakesh told her how Adil kept kicking him. She could see from the other bruises on his leg that somebody was certainly kicking him.

"Adil, did you kick Johnny?" Mrs Hilton asked him.

"I was only after the ball. It was an accident," he protested.

"It was not," said Johnny, finally standing up for himself. "He's always kicking me when I haven't got the ball." His two friends agreed with him. They said that ever since Adil arrived at the school he was always having a go at Johnny.

Mrs Hilton looked at Adil. It was unlikely that the other boys were lying and she had never seen Johnny this upset before.

"I think you had better come in and get that leg cleaned up, Johnny. Adil, you can stand outside Mr Hall's office. I'll deal with you later."

PARENTS

Many children are frightened to admit they are being bullied. They think that by complaining the situation might become worse. In this story Johnny was hoping that Adil would get tired of kicking him and stop. Here are some questions for you to discuss with your child:

1. *When should Johnny have told somebody that he was being kicked?*
2. *How did Johnny's friends, Mark and Prakesh, help him?*
3. *How did Johnny feel when he was being bullied by Adil?*
4. *How could you help if a friend of yours was being bullied?*

Activity:

Talk about the people your child could turn to, both at school and at home, if he or she is being bullied. Perhaps your child could pretend to be talking to one of them and practise what they would say.